T0346305

Grammar Book

Yvette Roberts and Aaron Jolly

Contents

1 What's this?

1 Read and chant. Who does Jack meet?

Hi, I'm Jack. What's your name?
My name is Ann. It's great to meet you.
Welcome, Ann. Welcome to our school.
Thank you, Jack. Your school is cool.

What's this? It's a crayon.
What's this? It's an eraser.
Welcome, Ann. Welcome to our school.
Thank you, Jack. Your school is cool.

2 What's this? Read and match.

1

A It's a backpack.

2

B It's a chair.

3

C It's an eraser.

3 Read again. Circle *is* and *'s*.

Grammar

What**'s** your name?	What**'s** this?
My name **is** Ann.	It**'s** a pencil.

4 Look and choose.

1 *Is / It's* a pen.　　**2** *It's / Is* a ruler.　　**3** *It's / It* a crayon.

5 Complete the questions.

1 A: .... this?

B: It's a desk.

2 A: .... your name?

B: My name is Carol.

6 Read and complete.

> a　is　It　s

1 My name .... Mrs. Brown.

2 What' .... this?

3 .... 's a marker.

4 It's .... ruler.

7 Play a guessing game. Choose things in the classroom. Ask, *What's this?*

What's this?

It's a pen.

1 Look. Label the colors and shapes.

What color is it?

> blue   green   purple   red

What shape is it?

> circle   rectangle   square   triangle

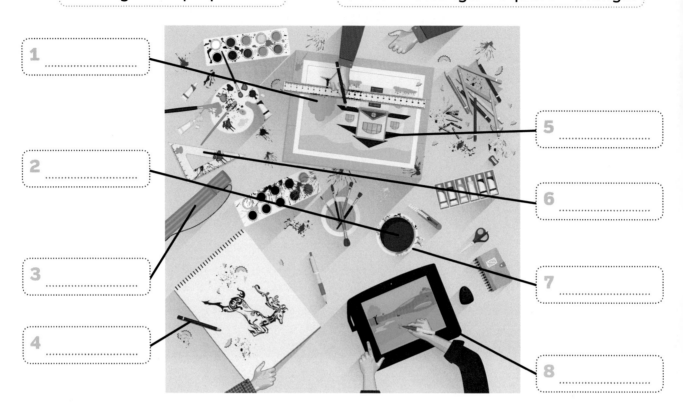

1 ....
2 ....
3 ....
4 ....
5 ....
6 ....
7 ....
8 ....

2 Read and choose.

1 Is this a square?
No, it isn't. / Yes,
it is.

2 What shape is it?
It's a triangle. / It's
a rectangle.

3 Is it red?
Yes, it is. / No,
it isn't.

Grammar

This is a pencil.	
Is this a pencil? Yes, it is. / No, it isn't.	What color is it? It's purple.
Is it blue? Yes, it is. / No, it isn't.	What shape is it? It's a square.

3 Read the grammar table again. Underline *this is*
and *it's*.

4 Look and match.

1 Is this a book?
2 What shape is it?
3 Is it green?
4 What color is it?

A No, it isn't.
B Yes, it is.
C It's red.
D It's a rectangle.

5 Put the words in order. Make questions and answers.

it Is Yes, is green it

1 ....? ....

isn't this it chair a No, Is

2 ....? ....

6 Look and complete.

is it It's It isn't It's

1 .... a book.
2 .... a backpack.
3 What color ....? .... yellow.

7 Choose things in the classroom. Ask and answer with a friend.

What color is it?
It's green.

What shape is it?
It's a circle.

Is this a marker?
Yes, it is.

Is it yellow?
No, it isn't.

1 Read. Who are they?

My favorite photo

Hi, I'm Zane. I am very happy. It's my birthday. I'm seven today. This is my family.

This is my sister, Jade. She's six years old.

Who is she?
She's my mother. She's funny.

Who is he?
He's my father. He's kind.

Who are they?
They're my grandmother and grandfather. They're great! They love me, too.

2 Read again and choose.

1   Who is she?

   A brother   **B** mother

2   Who is he?

   A father   **B** sister

3   He's seven. Who is he?

   A Jade   **B** Zane

Grammar

This is my father.
This isn't my mother.

Who is she?	Who is he?
She is my sister. / She's my sister.	He is my brother. / He's my brother.

Who are they?

They are my grandmother and grandfather. / They're my grandmother and grandfather.

3 Read again. Underline *she's*, *he's*, and *they're*.

4 Read and check (✔).

1 Who is this?
    A This isn't my grandmother. ☐   **B** This is my grandmother. ☐

2 **A** Who is she? ☐   **B** Who is he? ☐
    This is my mother.

3 **A** Who are they? ☐   **B** Who is she? ☐
    They are my cousins.

5 Which one is different?

1 She is my sister.   2   They are my brothers.   3   He is my grandfather.

6 Look at the answers. Write the questions.

1 .... ?   She is my sister.
2 .... ?   They are my grandfather and grandmother.
3 .... ?   He's my brother.
4 .... ?   They are my cousins.

7 Draw your family. Label the picture.

This is my family. This is my ....

This is ....
....

This ....
....

....
....

....
....

4 Read. Listen. Write!

1 Read and chant. Find two actions.

Good morning, class.
Open your books.
It's time to learn.
Read. Listen. Write!
Read. Listen. Write!
It's time to learn.

Good afternoon, class.
Close your books.
It's playtime.
Don't shout. Don't push.
Don't shout. Don't push.
It's playtime.

Goodbye, class.
Close your books.
It's time to go home.
Close your books.
Close your books.
It's time to go home.

● Our Class Rules ●

Read. Listen. Write!

Don't shout. Don't push.

2 Read again and match.

1 Read.

2 Don't push!

3 Don't run!

A

B

C

3 Read again. Underline _read_ in blue, _don't_ in red, and _write_ in green.

4 Read and circle the correct word.

1 Don't do this!   Read / Push / Listen

2 Do this!   Draw / Push / Shout

3 Don't do this!   Open your books / Read / Shout

4 Do this!   Push / Write / Shout

Grammar

Open / Close your books.
Listen. / Read. / Write. / Draw.
Don't shout.
Don't push.

10

5 What's different?

1 Don't shout.
   Don't shout!

2 Walk!
   Walk.

6 Look and choose. Write the rules.

listen / run / read

....

draw / push / shout

....

listen / shout / run

....

7 Work with a friend. Write five classroom rules. Use the words below.

close your books   draw   listen   open your books   push   run   shout

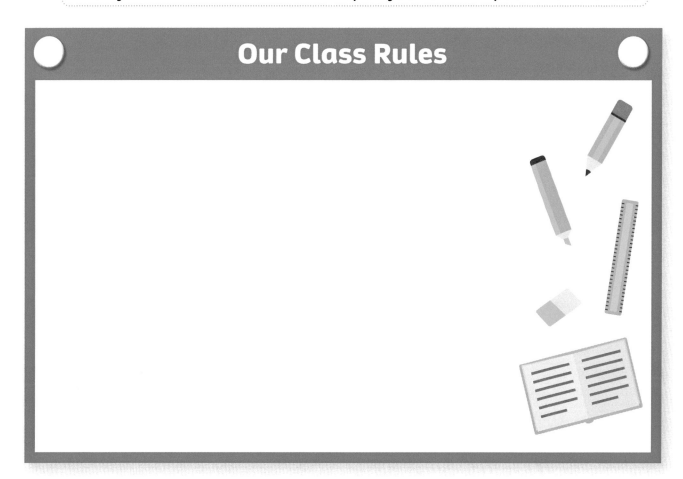

Our Class Rules

5 There are horses on the farm

1 **Read and look. Who is Max?**

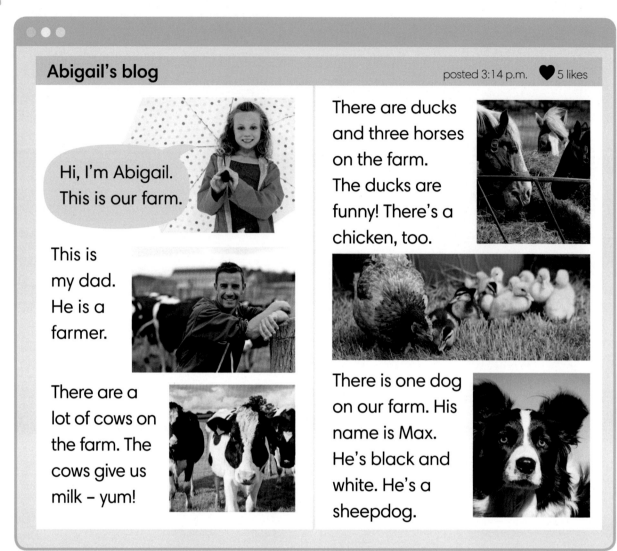

Abigail's blog posted 3:14 p.m. ♥ 5 likes

Hi, I'm Abigail. This is our farm.

This is my dad. He is a farmer.

There are a lot of cows on the farm. The cows give us milk – yum!

There are ducks and three horses on the farm. The ducks are funny! There's a chicken, too.

There is one dog on our farm. His name is Max. He's black and white. He's a sheepdog.

2 **Read again and write *Yes* or *No*.**

1   There are two dogs on the farm.   ....

2   There are horses on the farm.   ....

3   There is one cow on the farm.   ....

3 **Read again. Underline *there is* and *there's* in green, and *there are* in blue.**

Grammar

There is a dog. / There's a dog.

There is an ostrich. / There's an ostrich.

There are three horses.

4 Read and choose.

1 There *is / are* two frogs.

2 There *are / is* one goat.

3 There are three *cows / cow*.

4 There is *duck / a duck*.

5 There *are / is* two cats.

6 There is *a ostrich / an ostrich*.

5 Circle and write the correct letter.

n	t	s

There are three horse .... on the farm.

6 Read and complete.

a   an   are   is   There

1 There _____ one duck on the farm.

2 There _____ eight cows on the farm.

3 There is _____ ostrich on the farm.

4 _____ are three chickens on the farm.

5 There is _____ horse on the farm.

7 Draw a farm. Tell a friend. Then your friend draws it.

There are three horses on my farm. There is one ostrich, too.

OK. Next, please.

6 She's a black and white cat

1 Read and look. What animals can you see?

Come and visit the County Pet Shelter!
There are a lot of animals here.

Thor

This is Thor. Thor's a black dog. He's strong and friendly.

Pebble

Pebble's a cat. She's gray and white. She's cute!

Chalk and Cheese

Chalk and Cheese are two rabbits. They're brother and sister. They're gray rabbits. They're cute!

Scooby

Scooby's a hamster. He's a brown and white hamster. He's always hungry!

2 Read again. Write the animals.

1 They are gray. ....
2 She's gray and white. ....
3 He's black and strong. ....
4 He's brown and white. ....

3 Read again. Underline words which describe things.

4 Look and match.

1 It's a	A	brown turtles.
2 They're	B	black and white cows.
3 They're	C	green and red frog.

14

5 Read and complete.

a	a	s	s

1 It's .... black and white sheep.

2 They're cute cat ....

3 They're brown rabbit ....

4 It's .... black horse.

6 Look and say with a friend. Use *It's* or *They're*.

It's a brown chicken.

7 Look at the picture. Make a brochure for a pet shelter. Use Activity 1 to help you.

Greenpark Pet Shelter

....

They're ....

....

....

....

....

....

....

7 This is my family

1 Read and look. How many people are in the family?

I'm Todd, from New York. Here's my family.
There are a lot of us here, so count with me!

There's my mom, Malia. She's forty.
There's Tyler, my brother. He's thirteen.

My dad Jeff is here. He's forty-three.
Here are my sisters. They're nine, twelve, and fifteen.

I'm Todd, from New York. Here's my family.
There are a lot of us here, so count with me!

Three sisters, two brothers, one father and mother.
Our family is great. We look after each other!

2 Read again and circle T (*true*) or F (*false*).

1   There are two sisters.   T / F
2   There is one mother.   T / F
3   This is a small family.   T / F

3 Read again. Underline *'m*, *are*, and *'re*.

Grammar

I'm (am) Todd.	I'm not from Chicago.
You're (are) my sister.	You aren't my cousin.
He's/She's/It's (is) tall.	He/She/It isn't kind.
We're/You're/They're (are) a family.	We/You/They aren't brothers.

4 Read and choose.

1   They *isn't / aren't* my cousins. They are my brothers.
2   She *is / are* my grandmother.
3   He *isn't / aren't* my father. He's my grandfather.
4   They *is / are* my sisters.

5 Match.

1 **I am**	A **She's**
2 **You are**	B **They're**
3 **She is**	C **We're**
4 **We are**	D **You're**
5 **They are**	E **I'm**

6 Read and complete.

aren't He's is isn't She's

This is my family. They are great! My family is small, it **(1)** _____ big.
This **(2)** _____ my mother. **(3)** _____ smart and calm. Her
name is Rita. This is my father. **(4)** _____ funny. His name is Joseph.
My sisters are cool! They are funny, but they **(5)** _____ always nice!

7 Imagine this is your family. Tell a friend.

Grandfather – Jack, kind, polite

Grandmother – Bonnie, funny, smart

Me – Sunny, helpful, neat

Brother – Jacob, kind, funny

This is my family. He's my brother, Jacob. He's...

8 I have two legs

1 Read. How many parts of the body can you find?

Your Body
Do you have eight or ten toes?
Find out with Doctor Louisa!

Our bodies are amazing. You have one head. I have one head, too. I'm Doctor Louisa, and I'm just like you!

You have two strong arms and two hands. You have five fingers on each hand. They are good for drawing.

You don't have three feet. You have two feet. You have five toes on each foot. They are good for walking.

You have two eyes, one mouth, one nose, and two ears.

You have two strong legs. One leg, two legs. They are good for running!

2 How many? Put the words in the correct boxes.

arms   ears   eyes   fingers   hands   legs   mouth   nose   toes

One	Two	Ten
....	....	....
....	....	....
	....	

Grammar

I **have** one head.	I **don't have** three arms.	
You **have** two ears.	You **don't have** two fingers.	
We/You/They **have** one nose.	We/You/They **don't have** four legs.	
Do you **have** one mouth?	Yes, I **do**.	No, I **don't**.

3 Read again. Underline *have* and *don't have*.

4 Read and circle T (*true*) or F (*false*).

1 Do you have three ears? Yes, I do.   T / F

2 I don't have six fingers.   T / F

3 I have two mouths.   T / F

4 Do you have five arms? No, I don't.   T / F

5 What's similar?

1 I have two brothers.

2 I have two ears.

6 Look at the answers. Write the questions.

Do you have four arms ?

No, I don't have four arms. I have two arms.

1 _____ ?

Yes, I do. I have two feet.

2 _____ ?

No, I don't have seven fingers. I have ten fingers.

3 _____ ?

No, I don't have twelve toes. I have ten toes.

4 _____ ?

Yes, I do. I have one head.

7 Draw a monster in your notebook. Label the monster's body parts. Then tell a friend.

Do you have three arms?

No, I don't. I have three legs.

1 Read and match.

Robot Riddles

A

B

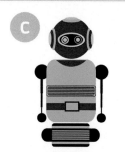
C

1 Beep

Does it have legs?

No, it doesn't. But it has two long arms.

Does it have a mouth?

No, it doesn't. But it has small eyes.

It has small eyes. Yes, it has small eyes.

2 Bop

Does it have ears?

It has two big ears. It has two big eyes.

Does it have a head?

It has one head. It doesn't have arms – surprise!

It doesn't have arms – surprise, surprise!

3 Bubba

Does it have toes?

No, it doesn't. No, it doesn't.

Does it have a mouth?

Yes, it does, but it doesn't have a nose.

It doesn't have a nose. No, it doesn't have a nose.

2 Read again and circle **T** (*true*) or **F** (*false*).

1 Beep doesn't have two arms. T / F
2 Beep doesn't have big eyes. T / F
3 Bop has three ears. T / F
4 Bubba has one mouth. T / F

Grammar

He has three eyes.	He doesn't have three eyes.
She has two feet.	She doesn't have two feet.
It has one leg.	It doesn't have one leg.

Does she have two hands?	Yes, she does.	No, she doesn't.

3 Read again. Underline <u>*has*</u> in pink, <u>*have*</u> in green, and <u>*doesn't*</u> in blue.

4 Match.

1 He doesn't   A   have eight fingers?

2 It   B   he does.

3 Does she   C   have one leg.

4 Yes,   D   has two hands.

5 What's different?

1 It has legs.

2 It doesn't have long legs.

3 Does it have legs?

6 Look and complete.

Does   does   doesn't   has   have   doesn't

1 Does it have a small head? Yes, it _____ .

2 It _____ have two legs.

3 _____ it have a nose? No, it doesn't.

4 It _____ two long legs.

5 Does it _____ brown ears? Yes, it does.

6 It _____ have fingers.

7 Work with a friend. Design a new toy and write about it. Then tell the class.

Here is our toy alien. His name is Zig Zag. He has three heads and six eyes. He has…

_____

_____

_____

_____

(10) Where's the gift?

1 Read and look. Where's the gift?

Sandro: Mom! Mom!

Mom: Sandro, what's wrong?

Sandro: Mom, where's my gift?

Mom: I don't know. Let's look for it.

Sandro: Hmm… It isn't on the bed.

Mom: Is it under the bed?

Sandro: No, it isn't… and it isn't on the desk.

Mom: Is it next to the chair?

Sandro: No, it isn't… and it isn't on the chair or under the chair.

Mom: Is it behind the closet?

Sandro: No, Mom. It isn't. Maybe it's in the closet… No, it isn't there. Mom!

Mom: Don't worry, Sandro. I can see it. It's on the closet.

Sandro: Thanks, Mom! You're awesome!

Mom: You're welcome.

2 Where does Sandro look? Read again and check (✔).

on the desk ⬭   under the chair ⬭   under the closet ⬭

in the closet ⬭   behind the desk ⬭   next to the chair ⬭

Grammar

Where's the ball?

in	under	behind	on	next to

3 Read again. Underline *on*, *next to*, *under*, *in*, and *behind*.

4 Look at the picture in Activity 1. Read and choose.

1 The teddy bear is *on / under / next to* the bed.

2 The desk is *behind / on / under* the window.

3 The lamp is *under / next to / on* the desk.

4 The yellow and orange flower is *on / in / next to* the shelf.

5 💡 **How many sentences can you make?**

book   toy box   couch   crayon

on   under   behind   is   the

The book is on the couch.

....

....

....

6 **Look at the image. Ask and answer with a friend.**

bedroom

bathroom

living room

kitchen

Where is the table?

It's in the kitchen.

7 🖍 **Look at the image in Activity 6. Choose one room. Write about it.**

The bedroom is big. The blue ball is next to the basket. The teddy is in the basket.

....

....

....

....

1 **Read. How many cows are on the farm?**

This is my grandfather and grandmother. They are on their farm. It's a beautiful day. There's an animal behind my grandfather. It's a big cow. There are three chickens next to my grandmother. There are two goats. I'm next to the calf. There's a red tractor behind me. Behind us is a house. It's small. There's a big tree next to it.

My grandfather always tells me what to do. "Don't run!" he says, "Close the door! Open the gate! Catch the calf!"

2 **Read again and write *Yes* or *No*.**

1   There is a cow next to my grandfather.   ....

2   There are two chickens next to my grandmother.   ....

3   There is a house next to the tree.   ....

4   It's a big house.   ....

5   My grandfather says "Close the door."   ....

3 **Read again. Underline *behind* and *next to*.**

4 **Read and choose.**

1   There *is / are* a black dog in the garden.

2   There *is / are* some chickens.

3   There is *a / an* orange chicken next to my grandmother.

4   *"Don't run," / "Not run,"* says my grandfather.

5   There is *a / an* house on the hill.

24

5 Read and complete.

behind   next   An   little   A

1. A _____ tree is next to the car.
2. _____ orange chicken is under the table.
3. The cow is _____ to the goat.
4. _____ black cat is on the chair.
5. The big horse is _____ the barn.

6 Put the words in order. Then match with a picture.

1. door   the   Open

   _____ . ◯

2. Close   gate   the

   _____ . ◯

3. run   Don't

   _____ . ◯

4. Open   books   your

   _____ . ◯

5. talk   Don't

   _____ . ◯

7 Work with a friend. Write five sentences about the picture.

There is a brown dog next to the girl.

1. _____ .
2. _____ .
3. _____ .
4. _____ .
5. _____ .

12 I can swim

1 Read. What sports are at the Sport Stars club?

Sam: Hi Marco. Look at this! Sport Stars club.

Marco: Sport Stars club. Hmm... fun! Can you swim?

Sam: Yes, I can. Can you?

Marco: Yes, I can.

Sam: Can you run?

Marco: Yes, I can. Can you?

Sam: Yes, I can run, too. Can you play basketball?

Marco: No, I can't.

Sam: Can you skate?

Marco: No, I can't...

Sam: And I can't skate... Look – soccer! You can play soccer!

Marco: Yes! And you can, too. You're great!

Sam: Thanks. Let's go to the club together!

⭐ SPORT STARS ⭐

Can you swim?

Can you run?

Can you play basketball?

Can you skate?

Can you play soccer?

Come and join the Sport Stars club! Wednesdays at 4 o'clock.

2 Read and circle T (*true*) or F (*false*).

1	Sam and Marco can swim.	T / F
2	Marco can't run.	T / F
3	Marco can't play basketball.	T / F
4	Sam can skate.	T / F

Grammar

I can jump.	I can't jump.
You can swim.	You can't swim.
He/She/It can run.	He/She/It can't run.
We/You/They can dance.	We/You/They can't dance.

Can you skate?	Yes, I can.	No, I can't.

3 Read again. Underline one sentence with *can*, one sentence with *can't*, and one question with *can*.

4 **Read and match.**

1 She can skateboard.

2 I can't ride a bike.

3 We can dance.

4 He can ride a horse.

5 They can't play basketball.

A

B

5 💡 **What's different?**

1 Can you swim?

2 I can jump.

3 I can't play soccer.

6 **Look and complete with *can*, *can't*, and sports.**

Hi, I'm Tatiana. I love sports. I **(1)** ✔ ....

Soccer is my favorite sport! I **(2)** ✔ .... ,

too. I **(3)** ✔ .... and I **(4)** ✔ ....

 .... I **(5)** ✗ ....

7 💬 **Ask and answer with a friend.**
Use the words below.

> dance   play basketball   play soccer
> ride a bike   ride a horse   skate   skateboard

Can you skateboard?

No, I can't. But I can skate!

(13) I brush my teeth

1 **Read. Who is Ana?**

> ### Asil's blog
> posted: 3.14 p.m. ♥ 5 likes
>
> I'm Asil. I'm seven. This is my day.
>
> I get up in the morning. I brush my teeth and comb my hair. I get dressed for school. I have breakfast. I eat toast and yogurt. Yum! My sister eats yogurt, too. Then she brushes her teeth. My dad eats toast and drinks coffee. He makes his lunch. I walk to school with my dad and my sister, Ana. Then my dad walks to work. He works in an office.
>
>
>
> After school, I have a snack and do my homework. My dad helps me. He helps my sister, too. I watch TV and take a bath. I brush my teeth and go to bed. I read in bed. I'm tired! My dad goes to bed late. He isn't tired!

2 **Read again. Put the sentences in order using the numbers 1–5.**

A Asil takes a bath. ⬭

B Asil goes to bed. ⬭

C Asil walks to school. ⬭

D Asil does his homework. ⬭

E Asil combs his hair. ⬭

3 **Read again. Underline *walk* and *brush* in red. Underline *walks* and *brushes* in green.**

Grammar

I walk to school.	He/She/It walks to school.
I brush my teeth.	He/She/It brushes his teeth.
I go to school.	He/She/It goes to school.
I do my homework	He/She/It does homework.
I make lunch.	He/She/It makes lunch.

4 Read and choose.

1 I *go / goes* to school.
2 He *take / takes* a bath.
3 She *get / gets* dressed.
4 I *do / does* my homework.

5 What's different?

1 I walk to school.
2 He walks to school.
3 I make my lunch.
4 He makes his lunch.

6 Look and write about Toby's day. Use the words in the correct form.

> brush   draw   drink   go   have   read

1 Toby _____ breakfast.
2 He _____ a picture.
3 He _____ a book.
4 He _____ his teeth.
5 He _____ milk.
6 He _____ to bed.

7 Write about your day.

I'm Hyen and this is my day. I get up and have breakfast.
I eat cereal and drink orange juice. I...

....
....
....
....
....

(14) Do you like lemonade?

1 **Read. How many drinks are in the chant?**

Lemonade, lemonade, I like lemonade!
Orange juice? No, thanks! I just like lemonade!

Do you like milk? Do you like water?
No, I don't! No, I don't! I just like lemonade!

What about your mom? What about your mom?
Does she like lemonade? Does she like lemonade?

No, she doesn't. No, she doesn't like lemonade.
She just likes mango juice. She just likes mango juice!

What about your dad? What about your dad?
Does he like lemonade? Does he like lemonade?

No, he doesn't. No, he doesn't like lemonade.
He just likes apple juice. He just likes apple juice.

2 **Read and circle T (*true*) or F (*false*).**

1	The girl likes milk.	T / F
2	The girl likes lemonade.	T / F
3	Her mom likes lemonade.	T / F
4	Her mom doesn't like mango juice.	T / F
5	Her dad likes apple juice.	T / F

3 **Read again. Underline one sentence with *like* in blue, one sentence with *likes* in red, and one sentence with *doesn't like* in green.**

Grammar

I like pizza.	I don't like pizza.
You like pizza.	You don't like pizza.
He/She/It likes pizza.	He/She/It doesn't like pizza.
We/You/They like pizza.	We/You/They don't like pizza.

Do you like pizza?	Yes, I do.	No, I don't.
Does she like pizza?	Yes, she does.	No, she doesn't.

4 Read and match.

1 Do you   A   like burgers.
2 He doesn't   B   do.
3 Yes, I   C   doesn't like cake.
4 She   D   like ice cream?

5 Which letters are missing? Write.

1 .... you like salad?   2 I .... n't like hot dogs.
3 She .... esn't like spaghetti.

6 Look and write.

She / ✔ / melon   _She likes melon._

1 I / ✗ / pears   ....

2 We / ✗ / grapes   ....

3 He / ✗ / cake   ....

4 They / ✔ / oranges   ....

7 Put a check (✔) or a (✗) for you. Then ask two friends.

Do you like cake?

Yes, I do.

Me				

(15) Where do you live?

1 **Read. Who's the new student at school?**

Daisy:	Hi, are you new at school?
Kamil:	Yes, I am. I'm Kamil. What's your name?
Daisy:	I'm Daisy. Nice to meet you.
Kamil:	Nice to meet you too, Daisy. How old are you?
Daisy:	I'm seven. How old are you?
Kamil:	I'm eight.
Daisy:	What sports do you like, Kamil?
Kamil:	Well, I like soccer and basketball. I can swim, too.
Daisy:	I like soccer and basketball, too. Where do you live?
Kamil:	I live on Parkside Road. It's next to school.
Daisy:	And who takes you to school?
Kamil:	My grandmother takes me to school.
Daisy:	Oh. I walk to school with my dad. What food do you like?
Kamil:	I like rice and beans. I like pizza, too.
Daisy:	You're lucky! It's pizza for lunch at school today!

2 **Read again and choose.**

1	How old is Daisy?	**A**	seven years old	**B**	six years old
2	What sports does Kamil like?	**A**	baseball	**B**	soccer
3	Where does he live?	**A**	Parkroad Side	**B**	Parkside Road
4	Who takes him to school?	**A**	grandmother	**B**	mother

Grammar

What sports do you like?	I like basketball.
Where do you live?	I live on Parkside Road.
Who takes you to school?	My grandfather.

3 **Read again. Underline _where_ in red, _what_ in green, and _who_ in blue.**

4 Read and choose.

1 *Who / What / Where* sports do you like?

2 *Who / What / Where* do you live?

3 *Who / What / Where* walks to school with you?

4 *Who / What / Where* food do you like?

5 How many questions can you make?

Where   What   Who   do   takes

school   live   you   sports   like   to

6 Read and complete.

do   What   Who

Joanna: (1) _____ sports do you like?
Marta: I like basketball. And I can skateboard, too.
Joanna: Me too. Where **(2)** _____ you live?
Marta: I live on Green Road.
Joanna: Me too! **(3)** _____ do you live with?
Marta: I live with my mom, dad, grandmother, and grandfather.

7 Ask the questions to three friends and complete the table.

What's your name?	Where do you live?	What sports do you like?	What food do you like?

I have some questions for you. What's your name?

My name is Boris.

(16) What are you wearing?

1 **Read. Name the clothes.**

What are you wearing today? Are you wearing a coat?

Hi, I'm Tad. I live in England. Today I'm wearing a white shirt and shorts. I'm not wearing a coat today. It's hot. I'm wearing a hat. I'm wearing my favorite sneakers, too. They're black and white.

Hello, I'm Demi. I live in Canada. It's very cold here. I'm not wearing a T-shirt and I'm not wearing shorts today! I'm wearing a coat. It's blue, white, and brown. I'm wearing gloves. I'm wearing a hat, too.

I'm Jayden. I live in the United States. I'm wearing a shirt. I'm wearing jeans and a sweater. I'm not wearing a hat. I'm not wearing a coat. I play basketball, so I'm not cold!

2 **Read again and choose.**

1 Who is wearing a white shirt?   Tad / Jayden

2 Who is wearing a sweater?   Demi / Jayden

3 Who is wearing a hat?   Tad and Jayden / Tad and Demi

4 Who is wearing a coat?   Demi / Jayden

Grammar

I'm wearing boots.	I'm not wearing a hat.
You're wearing a T-shirt.	You aren't wearing a jacket.
We/You/They're wearing gloves.	We/You/They aren't wearing shorts.

Are you wearing a sweater?	Yes, I am.	No, I'm not.

3 **Read again. Underline one sentence with _wearing_ and one sentence with _not wearing_.**

4 **Look at your clothes. Circle what is T (*true*) or F (*false*) for you.**

1 I'm wearing a shirt.   T / F

2 I'm wearing boots.   T / F

3 I'm not wearing a dress.   T / F

4 I'm not wearing jeans.   T / F

5 **Which letters are missing? Write.**

1 I'm wear .... a pink coat.

2 I'm not wear .... a skirt.

3 Are you wear .... a shirt?

6 **Read and complete.**

> are   I'm   'm   not   wearing

Hi Auntie Ella,

How are you? I live in Australia now. Today **(1)** .... wearing a pink T-shirt. It's my favorite T-shirt. I'm not **(2)** .... jeans. I'm wearing a pink skirt. I love pink! I **(3)** .... wearing my white sneakers, too. I'm **(4)** .... wearing a jacket. It's hot here! What **(5)** .... you wearing today?

Love,

Vicky

7 **What are you wearing? Draw and write.**

Today I'm wearing a blue shirt. I'm wearing red shorts. I'm not wearing a coat. It's hot today.

....

....

....

....

....

1 Read and look. Who is in Miss Green's class?

Look at Sam, Brooke, and Taylor. They are reading a book together. They are in the school library. Brooke and Taylor are smiling. They like the story. Sam isn't smiling!

Here are Molly, Lucy, Candy, and Florence. They are busy! They are in the classroom. They have colored pencils and paper. They aren't writing. They are drawing. They are drawing pictures of animals. Good work, girls!

This is Austin. He's on the school playground. He isn't playing soccer today. He has a basketball. He's playing basketball. He's smiling. Austin loves basketball.

Come and visit Miss Green's class! It's amazing!

Grammar

What is he/she doing?	What are they doing?
He/She is drawing.	They are reading.
He/She isn't listening.	They aren't singing.

2 Read again and match.

1 Sam is
2 Brooke and Taylor are
3 Florence is
4 Austin is

A playing basketball.
B smiling.
C drawing.
D reading with Brooke and Taylor.

3 Read again. Underline sentences with *reading*, *playing*, and *drawing*.

4 Read and choose.

1 They *isn't / aren't* drawing pictures of their family.

2 Ali is *write / writing* sentences.

3 Daisy and Wera *is / are* painting pictures of animals.

4 The teacher *isn't / aren't* running.

5 Read and circle the correct picture.

1 My brother and sister are walking to school.

2 Mr. Black is singing a song.

3 She is drawing a picture.

6 Read and complete. Ari and his grandfather are on the phone.

are   eating   're   reading   'm

Grandfather: Hi, Ari! What **(1)** .... you doing?

Ari: Grandfather! I'm in the living room. I'm **(2)** .... a book. What about you?

Grandfather: I'm **(3)** .... my lunch. I **(4)** .... eating salad. Where are your mom and dad? Are they reading?

Ari: No, they're in the kitchen. They **(5)** .... cooking dinner.

Grandfather: Great, their food is delicious! See you tomorrow, Ari!

7 Imagine your friends are doing different activities. Write five sentences about them.

eat   cook   draw   read   play basketball   play soccer   skate
skateboard   sing   walk

This is my class. Charley is reading a book. Jake and Sophia are...

1   Read. Who is playing hide and seek?

Teacher: Hi, Sasha. Who are you playing with today?

Sasha: Nobody. I'm looking for Ronnie.

Teacher: OK, let's look for Ronnie… Cody and Bradley are throwing and catching a ball.

Sasha: Hmm… What's Ant doing?

Teacher: He's playing soccer.

Sasha: Who is he playing with?

Teacher: He's playing with Rosie and Joe. They're fast!

Sasha: What are Mia and Abi doing?

Teacher: They're playing hide and seek.

Sasha: Where is Abi hiding?

Teacher: She's hiding next to the bikes.

Sasha: That's fun… and Ronnie? What's Ronnie doing?

Teacher: I can't see Ronnie. I know, let's look here…

Sasha: Ronnie, where are you?

Ronnie: Shh, I'm here! I'm hiding!

Sasha: Are you playing hide and seek, too?

Ronnie: Yes, come on! Hide here!

Sasha: Thanks! I love hide and seek.

Teacher: Bye, Sasha. Have fun!

2   Read again and write *Yes* or *No*.

1   Ant is playing basketball.   ....

2   Mia and Abi are throwing and catching.   ....

3   Abi is hiding next to the bikes.   ....

4   Ronnie is playing hide and seek.   ....

3   Read again. Underline *what*, *who*, and *where*.

Grammar

Where am I going?

Who are you playing with?

Where is he/she/it hiding?

What are we/you/they wearing?

4 Read and match.

1 What is he doing?   A They are playing with Matthew.

2 What is she doing?   B They are hiding in the toy box.

3 Where are they hiding?   C She is jumping.

4 Who are they playing with?   D He is riding a bike.

5 Put the words in order.

1 are What doing they .... ?

2 Where hiding she is .... ?

3 you What doing are .... ?

6 Look at the answers. Write the questions.

What is he doing ?
....
He is drawing.

1 .... ?

I'm playing hide and seek.

2 .... ?

They're swimming.

3 .... ?

She's playing with Jessica.

7 Look at the picture. Ask and answer.

What/the boy/doing?

1 What/the girl/doing?

2 What/the boy/wearing?

3 Who/the girl/running with?

4 What/the girl/wearing?

What is the boy doing?

He is running. He is smiling, too.

1 Read and look. What animals are on the farm?

Come and visit Big City Farm!

This is Big City Farm! Our farm is in the U.K., near a big city. We have so many animals for you to meet. My name is Daisy. I live on the farm with my mother and father. I love the animals. I help to feed them every day!

This is my horse. He's called Bunty. He's white. He's very fast and very strong. He's six years old and he's tall!

These are our geese. We have a lot of geese. They are white and they have orange

beaks. But that goose is gray with an orange beak. They all live next to our pond. The geese are noisy!

That is our prize cow. Her name is Gertrude. She's brown and she's beautiful. She eats a lot of grass!

Those are our sheep. They're white and they have black heads. They're very friendly.

2 Read again. Write the animals.

1   He is white and tall. ....

2   She is brown and beautiful. ....

3   They are white and they have black heads. ....

3 Read again. Underline *this*, *that*, *these*, and *those*.

Grammar

This is my horse.	**These** are **geese**.
That is a cow.	**Those** are **sheep**.

4 Read and choose.

1   This is *a frog / frogs*.

2   These are my *duck / ducks*.

3   *This / These* are the horses.

4   *That / These* is the goat.

5 Put the words in the correct bubble.

> fish   fish   geese   goose   horses   horse
> mouse   mice   sheep   sheep

one

....

....

....

....

....

two or more

....

....

....

....

....

6 Look and complete.

This .... _is_ .... _my cat._

1 .... a goat.

2 .... my pet mice.

3 .... sheep.

7 Look at the picture. Point and say.

That is a chicken.

Those are chickens.

(20) Can I play with you?

1 **Read. Who is playing with the toys?**

Look at me! Look at me! I'm playing with my toys!
Look at me! Look at me! I'm playing with girls and boys!
Shall we play with blocks? Let's ask Ben and Asher.
And what about Gemma? Let's ask her.

Look at me! Look at me! I'm playing with my toys!
Look at me! Look at me! I'm playing with girls and boys!
Are you playing hide and seek? I can see you!
Are you playing hide and seek? Can I play, too?

Look at me! Look at me! I'm playing with my toys!
Look at me! Look at me! I'm playing with girls and boys!
Do you like my new blue car? You can play with it.
Do you like my action figure? Look at him – he sits!

Look at me! Look at me! I'm playing with my toys!
Look at me! Look at me! I'm playing with girls and boys!
I really love your trains. Can I play with them?
Oh no, playtime's over! We're out of time.

2 **Read again. Match the sentences from the chant.**

1 Look at   A   it.
2 I can see   B   them?
3 You can play with   C   you!
4 Can I play with   D   me!

3 **Read again. Underline the words** _me_, _her_, _it_, **and** _him_ **one time.**

4 **Read and match.**

1 There's Alicia.   A   I can see him.
2 Mark is next to the bikes.   B   Can I play with it?
3 I like your train.   C   Let's ask her to play.

Grammar

Look at me.
I can see you.
I can play with him.
Let's ask her.
You can play with it.
You can play with us.
I like you.
Can I play with them?

5 Read and circle the correct picture.

1 I like her.

2 Let's ask him.

3 I like it.

4 She skates with them.

6 Read and complete.

| her   it   us   them |

I'm Rocco. These are my toys.
These are my trains. I like
(1) _____. They are
different colors. I have an
action figure, too. I love
(2) _____. It's my
favorite toy.

I'm Lee. I play with my sister,
Penny. Penny is funny. I love
(3) _____. We live with our
mom, dad, grandmother,
and grandfather. They all love
(4) _____ very much.

7 Write about your toys or family.
Use *it/them/him/her*.

I'm Chen. I love my toys. This is my favorite airplane.
It's blue. I love it!

....

....

....

....

1 **Read. Who is hitting a ball? Who is riding a bike?**

It's Saturday afternoon at the park. A lot of things are happening!

These boys are playing baseball.

Liam is hitting the ball.

His friend Mason is catching the ball behind him.

Liam is wearing a blue T-shirt.

That child next to the tree is Mohammed. He is counting.

Those children are running away.

They are playing hide and seek.

These children are riding bikes. It's Gael and his brother Lucas.

These geese are flying.

This goose is eating.

These boys are watching soccer.

Those men are running and kicking the ball.

Those people are watching the soccer game.

These children are hiding. They are Elena and Leon.

Elena is wearing a blue T-shirt. Leon is wearing a red T-shirt. He is behind her.

2 **Read and circle T (*true*) or F (*false*).**

1   Liam is catching the ball.   T / F
2   Mohammed is counting.   T / F
3   Gael is riding his bike.   T / F
4   The geese are running.   T / F
5   Elena is wearing a red blouse.   T / F

3 **Read again. Underline sentences with *those*.**

4 Read and match.

1 What are those boys wearing?
2 Where is that girl going?
3 Where are these girls playing?
4 What are you doing?
5 Who is eating an apple?

A Malik is eating an apple.
B They are wearing hats.
C They are playing in the park.
D She is going to school.
E I'm doing my homework.

5 Read and complete.

her   it   him   us   me

1 My grandfather is smart. I like ....
2 My sister is funny. I love ....
3 The tractor is old. I don't like ....
4 We are in the garden. John is standing next to ....
5 It's my sandwich. It's for ....

6 Read and choose.

1 The *mouse / mice* are hiding.
2 Some *children / child* are playing soccer.
3 A *goose / geese* is drinking water.
4 A *child / children* is kicking a soccer ball.
5 There is a *mouse / mice* in the kitchen.

7 Talk about the picture with a friend. What are they doing?

That boy is riding a bike.

These children are swinging.

1 **Read. Who can sing?**

Meet Yi Ling and Reece!

Hi, I'm Yi Ling. I'm seven. This is my bedroom. I have a white bed and a pink closet.
I live with my mom and dad. We live in Singapore, in an apartment. We have a pet, too. His name is Walter. He's a black dog. I walk him every day after school.

I like basketball and I can ride a horse. I can dance, too. My favorite color is pink, but I'm wearing blue today! My favorite food is pizza. I like oranges and cake, too.

Hi, I'm Reece. I'm seven. In the picture I'm wearing a gray T-shirt and jeans – the same as my dad! We're making a salad for lunch.
I live with my dad and my grandmother. We live in Toronto, Canada. We live in a small house. We don't have a pet. I play basketball with my friends. I can sing but I can't dance. I can skate, too.

My favorite food is ice cream and burgers.

2 **Read again. Answer the questions.**

1 Who has a pet?

2 Who is wearing jeans and a gray T-shirt?

3 Who can't dance?

4 Who lives with their mother and father?

3 **Read again. Underline sentences with** *can*, *have*, **and** *like*.

4 **Read and circle.**

1 Dan *has / can / is* seven years old.

2 *Those / They / That* boys are swimming.

3 She *isn't / can't / doesn't like* apple juice.

4 What are you *do / doing / don't?*

5 Find and write the missing letters.

h n a t e n i e a i r

1 He c _____ _____ ride a bike.

2 I don't _____ a v _____ a brother.

3 The girls are w _____ _____ _____ _____ _____ g hats.

4 What are they e a _____ _____ n g?

6 Look and complete.

Name	Darren	Family	Mother, father, 2 sisters
Age	8	Sports	dance ✔ swim ✘
Lives	Sydney, Australia	Likes	apples, hot dogs, cake

1 His name _____ Darren.

2 He _____ in _____ , Australia.

3 He _____ two sisters.

4 He _____ dance. He _____ .

5 He _____ apples, _____ , and cake.

7 Write the questions. Then ask and answer with a friend.

Where/live?

Where do you live?

I live in a house.

I live in an apartment.

1 Who/live with?

2 What/have/in your bedroom?

3 Do/have/pet?

4 What/wearing today?

5 What sports/can/play?

6 What/food/like?

Vocabulary

Unit 1

backpack, chair, crayon, desk, eraser, marker, pen, ruler

Unit 2

blue, green, purple, red, yellow; shape, circle, rectangle, square, triangle

Unit 3

cousins, family, brother, father, grandmother, grandfather, mother, sister

Unit 4

close, draw, listen, open, push, read, run, shout, walk, write

Unit 5

cat, chicken, cow, dog, duck, farm, farmer, frog, goat, horse, ostrich

Unit 6

hamster, rabbit, turtle; black, brown, gray, white; cute, friendly, hungry

Unit 7

dad, mom; big, small; calm, cool, funny, helpful, kind, neat, nice, polite, smart

Unit 8

arm, body, ear, eye, fingers, foot, feet, hand, head, leg, mouth, nose, toes

Unit 9

arm, body, ear, eye, fingers, foot, feet, hand, head, leg, mouth, nose, toes

Unit 10

bathroom, bedroom, kitchen, living room; bed, chair, closet, desk, shelf, table, window

Unit 11

barn, car, door, farm, gate, house; calf, cow, chicken, goat

Unit 12

dance, jump, play basketball/soccer, ride a bike/horse, run, skate, swim

Unit 13

brush my teeth, comb my hair, do my homework, get dressed, go to bed, have breakfast, make my lunch, take a bath, walk to school, watch TV

Unit 14

apple juice, burger, cake, grapes, hot dog, ice cream, lemonade, mango juice, melon, milk, orange, orange juice, pear, pizza, salad, spaghetti

Unit 15

beans, pizza, rice; baseball, dad, mom, skateboard

Unit 16

boots, coat, dress, gloves, hat, jacket, jeans, shirt, shorts, skirt, sneakers, sweater, T-shirt

Unit 17

cooking, drawing, eating, reading a book, painting, singing, smiling, walking, writing

Unit 18

catching, hiding, jumping, playing, playing hide and seek, riding, throwing

Unit 19

fish, goose, geese, mouse, mice, sheep; cat, chicken, cow, duck, frog, horse

Unit 20

action figure, blocks, cars, toy

Unit 21

kicking the ball; flying, playing baseball, swinging, watching

Unit 22

apartment, bed, bedroom, closet, house; black, blue, gray, pink, white; apple, burger, cake, hot dog, ice cream, oranges, pizza, salad; jeans, pet, T-shirt